THIS BOOK BELONGS TO:

D0431248

Name: ....

Spirit animal: ....

Favorite place (in nature): ....

Your geographic
coordinates on Earth:

Please mail or recycle if found:

N___°___'_____"

W___°___'_____"

Right index fingerprint:

Address and other instructions:

....

....

....

....

....

....

\ \ \ \ \ \ \ ｜ / / / / / / /

While you enjoy this book, keep safe, respect the environment and the countryside codes, leaving only footprints behind.

/ / / / / ｜ \ \ \ \ \ \

Into Nature

A Creative Field Guide and Journal

Unplug and Reconnect with What Matters

The Mindfulness Project

THE EXPERIMENT

NEW YORK

Map of Contents

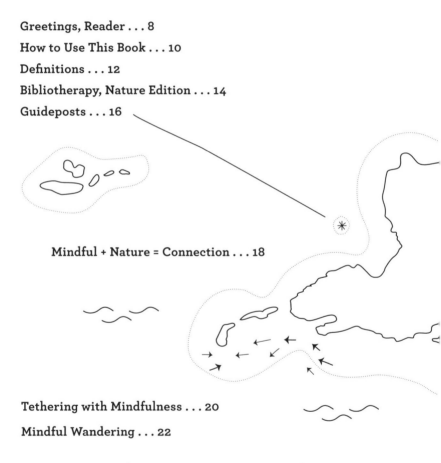

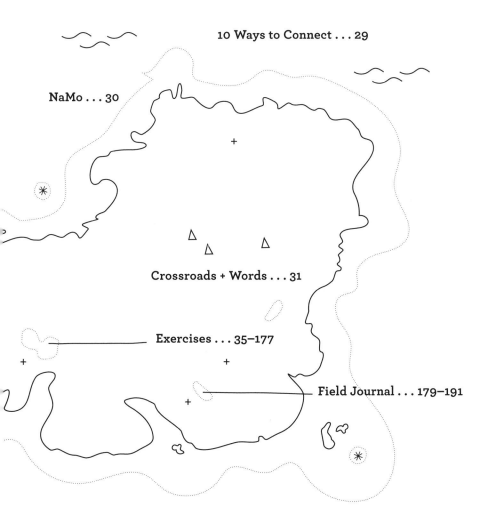

Exercise Log

Greetings, Reader

Congratulations on wanting to reconnect. Let this book be your guide, journal, and inspiration as you seek to explore nature in a meaningful way. Mindfulness will be your passport on this journey through the natural world. You don't have to go far. Nature is right here, all around us. We only need to slow down and awaken our senses, as well as our hearts, to really notice and engage with it.

It only takes a moment to look up at the sky, greet the wind on your cheeks, or tune in to the birdsong outside your window. Even just brief moments of connection with our senses and the little wonders of nature can remind us that we, too, belong to nature. And it's here that we can find the peace of mind and the soul-soothing renewal we truly need.

The collection of exercises in this book will help you seek nature in small ways. But you will also find a framework and the invitation to take longer excursions to really immerse yourself in nature. Disconnecting from our devices and reconnecting with ourselves on a regular basis – this is our wisest pursuit and really the ultimate luxury. You don't have to be the "outdoorsy" type (we certainly are not). Just go as you are, to the places that are accessible to you. Sit

down in the grass, walk through the woods, look out over the sea – start with the nature you know and then keep exploring.

Use mindfulness to stay grounded in the moment and connected with your breath as you take it all in. Nature itself is a profound mindfulness teacher. It can show us how to be still, how to be strong, how to go with the flow, and how to just be and let life unfold with gracious acceptance.

We hope you enjoy the journey, all the precious moments, and the sense of wonder that mindful nature connection will offer.

Happy mindful wandering and be well, wild thing.

:) The Mindfulness Project

How to Use
This Book

The book is designed as a field guide to exploring and connecting with nature in a fun and creative way. It includes instructions for excursions into the wild and exercises that will help you to connect with nature, right where you are.

Here are some suggestions on how to use it:

(1) The Introduction (pages 10–33) includes some important tips and ground rules.

(2) Keep the Guideposts (page 16) in mind while doing the exercises and exploring outdoors.

(3) Exercises don't need to be completed in any order.

(4) Adapt and make the exercises relevant to you.

(5) Some exercises, do more than once.

(6) Plan Mindful Wanderings (page 23) and use the Field Notes (pages 180–191) section to record your observations.

Fill these pages with your discoveries and insights along the way. Feel free to capture them in whatever way inspires you.

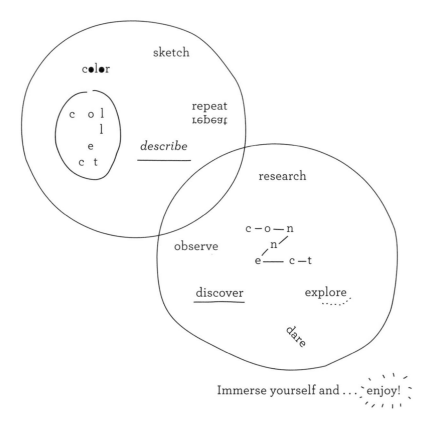

Definitions

MINDFULNESS

Mindfulness is about paying attention to our internal and external world with a kind and nonjudgmental awareness. Engaging all of our senses to connect with our present-moment experience without getting lost in thought or habitual distractions. It can be trained through meditation, but also practiced whenever and wherever we are.

MINDFUL NATURE CONNECTION

Using the skills and principles of mindfulness to engage with the natural world, with our senses awake and without striving to get somewhere or trying to understand everything on a cognitive level. Just allowing ourselves to simply be in nature and connect with the sense of wonder that it evokes.

It can be practiced for the enrichment of your health and well-being through any activity that puts you in contact with nature (indoors or out).

RELATED TERMS

— ECOTHERAPY
— NATURE THERAPY
— ECOPSYCHOLOGY ✳

✳ OIKOS = Home / PSYCHE = Soul / LOGOS = Knowledge

"Knowing that the earth is home to the soul."
John Seed and Tina Fields

Bibliotherapy, Nature Edition

It is easy to forget that poets, explorers, authors, and philosophers have been writing about nature connection for ages. Stock your shelves with a few of these inspiring reads.

Anything by Henry David Thoreau (**WALDEN, WALKING**)

WILD: FROM LOST TO FOUND ON THE PACIFIC CREST TRAIL   *Cheryl Strayed*

NATURE CURE   *Richard Mabey*

ESSENTIAL MUIR   *Fred D. White*

NATURE   *Ralph Waldo Emerson*

Anything by *Mary Oliver* (**WINTER HOURS, WEST WIND, UPSTREAM**)

THE HIDDEN LIFE OF TREES   *Peter Wohlleben*

Add more of your favorite titles here.

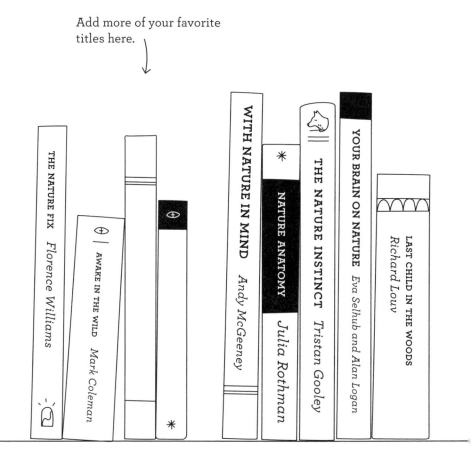

THE NATURE FIX *Florence Williams*

AWAKE IN THE WILD *Mark Coleman*

WITH NATURE IN MIND *Andy McGeeney*

NATURE ANATOMY *Julia Rothman*

THE NATURE INSTINCT *Tristan Gooley*

YOUR BRAIN ON NATURE *Eva Selhub and Alan Logan*

LAST CHILD IN THE WOODS *Richard Louv*

Guideposts

Mindful nature connection is an experiential concept. Here are some principles to help you find your way as you explore the exercises in this book and the natural world around you.

1. ANCHOR IN THE BODY

Let your body always be your home base. Gather your attention in any given moment by simply tuning in to the sensations of your body and breath. Practice this to ground yourself before and while you are connecting with nature. Your senses are the gateway to taking it all in. (See also Tethering on page 20.)

2. STAY CURIOUS

Explore the natural world with an open mind. Our tendency is often to race past everything we think we already know, but even the familiar can surprise you if you stay open to discovery. Try bringing an attitude of curiosity to each exercise and each encounter.

3. JUST BE

If you are not used to it, spending time in nature can feel like a waste of time, unless you are on your way somewhere. It will take practice to slow down and settle into just being in nature.

4. GO WITH THE FLOW

Sometimes the conditions of our experience in and with nature might not be exactly as we would like (e.g., weather, scenery, smells). Practice allowing and accepting things just as they are.

5. KNOW BY HEART

To connect with nature, you don't have to seek answers or comprehension. Just let it reveal itself to you in an experiential way, which offers a different way of knowing.

6. JUST TRUST

Trust your instincts and your inner wisdom. Recognize the interconnectedness of things and your place within it all, right here in this moment . . . and this one . . .

7. TAKE CARE

It is important to feel safe and comfortable when you engage with nature. Make your basic needs a priority. Ensure you are warm enough and have the necessary food/water, cushions, blankets, and information you need. Know your limits and be kind to yourself.

8. DON'T GET ATTACHED

Nature connection is sometimes profound and blissful, but try not to get attached to this outcome. We may not always have good feelings, and they can't be forced. All we can do is show up with the intention to be with and allow whatever experience we are having. And that can make all the difference.

9. STAY COMMITTED

Commit to getting into nature on a regular basis as an act of self-care. And also make a commitment to treating nature with care and respect.

10. SENSE WONDER

Contemplate the miracle of everything and savor the little moments of wonder and awe.

Mindful + Nature

The body is our vehicle for exploring our inner and outer worlds. Use mindfulness to be aware of the thoughts, feelings, and sensations within, as you engage with the natural world around you.

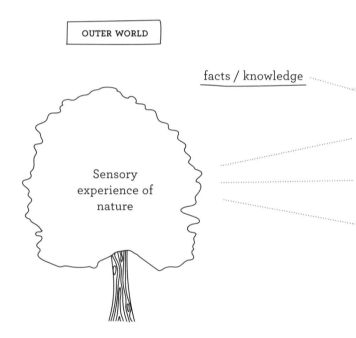

OUTER WORLD

facts / knowledge

Sensory
experience of
nature

= **Connection**

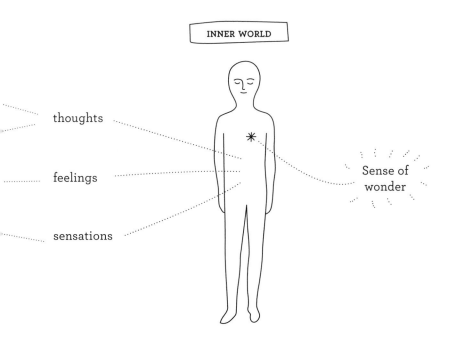

INNER WORLD

thoughts

feelings

sensations

Sense of
wonder

✳ Engaging with the natural world through mindfulness often
results in a sense of wonder that radiates love and connectedness,
creating truly magical moments.

Tethering

Use your body as a base from which to tether your attention out, as you explore nature. Feel what it feels like to be in your body – your feet on the ground, the flow of your breath, the sensations in your hands. Then practice shifting your focus between your inner and outer worlds.

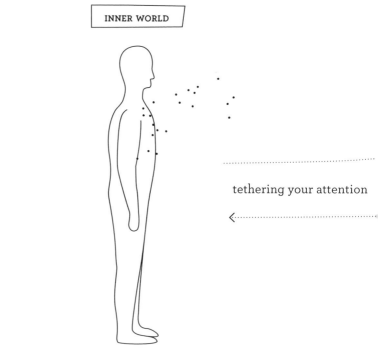

INNER WORLD

tethering your attention

with Mindfulness

Scan out and take in your external environment through the senses, then reconnect with your body. Back and forth. See if you can get to the point of holding it all in your awareness simultaneously.

OUTER WORLD

Mindful

To really get into nature, you need to go out and spend some time in the wild. As you start exploring off the beaten path, use this framework as your guide to connecting mindfully.

PERMISSION:

Give yourself permission to take time out, disconnected from your devices, to spend time in and be with nature.

INTENTION:

During your dedicated time outdoors, set the intention to connect and be present with the nature around you, as well as your internal experience. Be the observer or the field researcher of your inner and outer worlds.

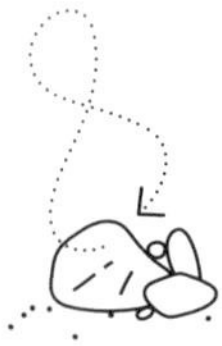

ATTENTION:

Rest your attention on the sensory experiences of nature – the smells, sights, sensations. And when the mind wanders, as it will, bring your attention gently back to your body or the object of your attention.

ATTITUDE:

Remember to follow the Guideposts and bring the qualities of mindfulness such as curiosity, allowing, and nonjudgmental awareness to your time in nature – this will enrich your experience with profound and insightful moments.

Wandering

From local or national parks to public footpaths, plan some routes and make a day of it.

Make your wander-list here:

....

....

....

....

....

....

....

....

....

....

p.s. You don't have to go far. Start where you are. Nature is at your doorstep :)

Follow the framework over the next few pages to really connect with nature on your wander routes. Use the Field Notes at the back of the book (page 180) to record your wanderings and findings.

Stay curious

Sight (10 mins.) Find an area a bit off your path to look around. First take some time to slowly look around you in all directions, taking it all in through your eyes, the colors, shades, movement and aliveness. Then start exploring things up close, noticing every little detail. Give them your full attention.

Smell (10 mins.) Tune in to your sense of smell as you continue on your way. Take in the scent of the air. Smell the leaves, trees, earth, and flowers, if you find them. Savor the aromas and feelings they evoke.

Taste (30 mins. – Lunch/Snack Break) Settle in to a comfortable place to enjoy your lunch or snack. Savor the taste and cultivate a sense of gratitude for all the effort it took to get the different ingredients to you.

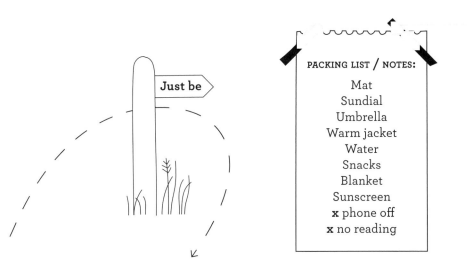

Just be

PACKING LIST / NOTES:

Mat
Sundial
Umbrella
Warm jacket
Water
Snacks
Blanket
Sunscreen
x phone off
x no reading

Sound (10 mins.) Explore sounds. Sit for a while and just listen, eyes closed. See if you can hear with your whole body, and try to relax into just receiving sounds, letting go of the labels and judgments about them. Just let them wash over you, resting in that silence between the sounds.

No phone

Go with the flow

Touch (10 mins.) Find a place just off the path to explore your sense of touch. Spend ten minutes here feeling things and tuning into the exact point where your senses meet their surface. Maybe sometimes closing your eyes, really sensing only by touch. When your mind wanders off, gently bring it back to the sensations.

Water (30 mins.) Sit and contemplate the element of water and all the ways water sustains nature. Consider how it is a part of all living things, including your own body. If you can sit down next to some sort of body of water, do. Observe its qualities: its movement and its stillness. As you sit, just be with your experience as it arises and notice how it flows through you.

Earth (30 mins.) The faithful companion, under our feet holding it all together. Find a comfortable place to sit, feeling grounded with your back against a tree. Consider all the life it's sustaining, all of the trees and plants growing from its nutritious soil. Not just here, but everywhere. Feeding us, working for us, providing shelter for us.

→ **Air (30 mins.)** This elusive element reveals itself within and around us. Observe how the wind moves through tall grasses and leafy treetops. Feel the air brushing your skin and traveling through your breathing body. Notice how air carries both sounds and scents from afar.

Know by heart

Trust, Sense, Wonder

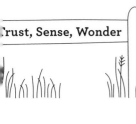

Fire/Sun (30 mins.) Reflect on this critical element and how it has allowed us to harness energy, generate warmth, grow food, light our days and nights, survive in the cold. Notice all the ways it is working right where you are, right now.

Sit still for a while.
In silence.
Eyes open.
Notice life around you.
Sense life within you.

Inspired by Margaret Kerr, Scotland.

"Rest is not idleness, and to lie sometimes on the grass under the trees on a summer's day, listening to the murmur of water, or watching the clouds float across the blue sky, is by no means a waste of time."

John Lubbock

10 Ways to Connect

Cut or tear out this page, stick it on the wall, put it in your wallet, take a photo, share it.*

1. Go outside and notice the nature right at your doorstep.

2. Meditate for at least five minutes – tuning in to your body and breath.

3. Tend to your houseplants or a garden.

4. Connect with a pet – your own or a neighbor's.

5. Contemplate the source of products and recycle.

6. Eat whole foods and savor them.

7. Look up at the sky, day and night.

8. Connect with the weather – wind on cheeks, raindrops on rooftops.

9. Practice gratitude for all that nature provides.

10. Connect with a tree and listen for birdsong.

Disconnect from your devices to maximize nature connection.

NaMo

Sometimes we need to make a conscious effort to stop what we are doing and drop into the moment to really connect with nature. Whether you are in the midst of a walk or on your daily routine, follow these tips for a nourishing "**Na**ture **Mo**ment."

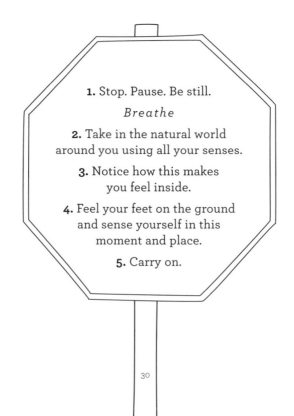

1. Stop. Pause. Be still.

Breathe

2. Take in the natural world around you using all your senses.

3. Notice how this makes you feel inside.

4. Feel your feet on the ground and sense yourself in this moment and place.

5. Carry on.

Crossroads + Words

"Two roads diverged in a wood, and I –
I took the one less traveled by,
And that has made all the difference."

Robert Frost

Complete this crossword puzzle, diverging paths in mind . . .

ACROSS

3. Nonjudgmental awareness of our inner and outer worlds:

_____

6. Maneuver to go back in the direction from which we came:
_ - ___.

7. Take a _____-_____ day, where you disconnect from your devices and reconnect with yourself and the world around you.

9. A feeling of peace of mind or being at ease.

10. Words of _____. Nature offers this and awakens it within you.

11. Adjective meaning "contains substance necessary for growth, health, and well-being."

12. "The Sound of _____": Simon & Garfunkel song from 1964.

13. _____ the world around you, like a curious child would.

DOWN

1. On the verge of a _____. When a candle loses its flame.

2. Color that is also a feeling: ____.

4. _____-_____ Disorder. A term coined by Richard Louv in 2005 to reflect the cost to our well-being from losing connection to the natural world.

5. _____ in thought. Opposite of being present.

7. Starts with "dis," ends with "d." Feeling detached.

8. _____ by work, by information, by artificial sensory stimulation.

Exercises

Follow

Animals have their own lives, little do we notice. Follow a bee, a bug, or a butterfly for a couple of moments of its life and make notes on your findings.

NOTES

Nature Niche

Choose a corner of your home to make a nature niche. Once a day, sit and just be among nature.

IDEAS

Potential locations: Living room, corner of bedroom . . .
Comfort: Cushion, chair, blanket, pillow, rug, mat . . .
Tools: Watering can, vase, matches, notebook . . .
Inspiration: Pine-scented candles, dried leaves, bark, rocks, photos of scenes you love, fresh flowers, houseplants, dried herbs . . .

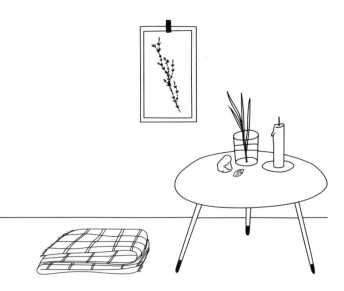

Place a photograph or sketch of your nature niche here.

Treasure Hunt

Wherever you go, keep an eye out for nature's treasures. Tick them off as you add them to your nature niche:

◯ Slate

◯ Pine cone

◯ Seashell

◯ Ladybug (to be set free)

◯ Acorn

◯ Wheat stalk

◯ Animal tracks (draw them here . . .)

◯ Birch bark

◯ Daisy

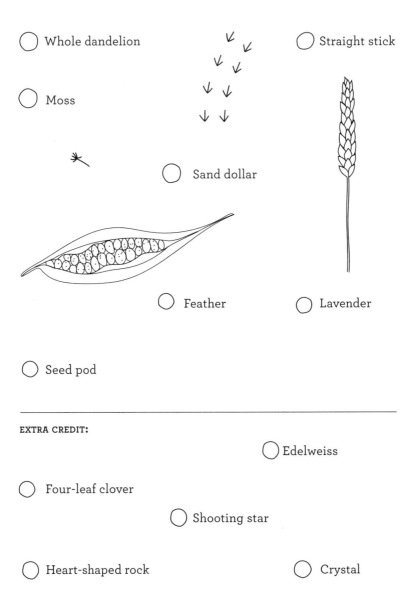

○ Whole dandelion

○ Moss

○ Sand dollar

○ Straight stick

○ Feather

○ Lavender

○ Seed pod

EXTRA CREDIT:

○ Edelweiss

○ Four-leaf clover

○ Shooting star

○ Heart-shaped rock

○ Crystal

Lay of the Land

Go to a place/area you enjoy being in nature (or a new place you wish to get to know), whether it be a park or a more wild setting.

	Trees		Flowers
	Mountains		Hideout
	River / Stream		Lookout
	Field		Animal tracks
	Walking trail		Structure
	Beach		Meditation spot
	Road		Rocks
	Animal sightings		Lake

Make a map of the area. Use the icons above to guide you or draw your own. Include the trees, streams, structures, viewpoints, hideouts, wildlife, and flowers – places where you had an insight and other beautiful things you noticed.

Pet Plant
Meditation

If a houseplant is as close to nature as you can come at the moment, then that is just fine.

Find a comfortable place to sit with your houseplant.

Close your eyes and feel the sensations of your in breath and your out breath. Don't worry if your mind wanders off. Just gently bring it back to sensing the breath.

Now, open your eyes.

Look at the plant. Its colors. The shape of its
leaves. Look at it from all sides.

Then start to explore the plant with your hands.
Touch its leaves. Its soil.

Now, smell the soil, then rub and smell its leaves.

Contemplate your plant. Think of the wonder
of it having grown out of the soil contained in
its planter, that it is here right now sharing the
space and air with you. Maybe thank it for the
joy it brings you and for its resilience, too.

Drawing Sounds

Find a place to sit somewhere outdoors in nature. Listen to the sounds around you. Maybe that includes birds, rustling leaves, cicadas in the bushes, a plane flying overhead, or voices . . . Draw each sound here and label it.

Pigeon

Cyclist

Crow cawing

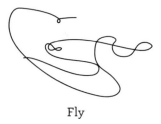

Fly

Repeat in different places. At the end of each session, just close your eyes and sit for 5 minutes . . . bathing in the orchestra of sounds.

* Footnotes

There are so many different surfaces to be found in nature: grass, rock, leaves, earth, sand, and . . . water!

Take off your shoes and mindfully walk on them, slowing down your pace.

How does it feel to . . .

. . . have grass bend beneath your steps?

. . . have mud between your toes?

... bury your feet in the sand?

... crunch over dried leaves?

... submerge your feet in a
stream or ocean waves?

... cling to the surface of a
rock with your toes?

Feathery Friends

Learn about the birds that are native to your area. Make a profile of a few of them here. Note their colors, special features, bird calls (with a phonetic example), and any fun facts.

PIGEON

NAME:

COLORS: GREY, WHITE, PINK

BIRD CALL: BRR BRR BRR

FUN FACT: THEY USED TO DELIVER MESSAGES OVER LONG DISTANCES

NICKNAME: PAMELA

COLORS:

BIRD CALL:

FUN FACT:

NICKNAME:

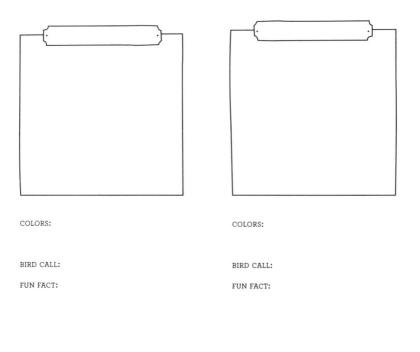

"Keep a green bough in your heart and a singing bird will come."

Lao Tzu

COLORS:

COLORS:

BIRD CALL:

FUN FACT:

BIRD CALL:

FUN FACT:

NICKNAME:

NICKNAME:

Nature + Nurture

Plant two seeds in two different pots. Provide both with the same amount of water, light, and nutrients. But once a day:

To one, only provide the basic care and keep it in a place where it gets less attention.

To the other, give love – speak to it in a kind voice, tend to it with care, smile at it, and maybe play it nice music.

What happens?

Exhibit 1

Exhibit 2

Tips for planting seeds:

STEP 1
Soak your seeds in water for a few hours in advance.

STEP 2
Fill your pot with potting soil.

STEP 3
Plant a few seeds three times as deep as the seeds are wide.

STEP 4
Place the pot in a sunny spot and water it as the soil starts to feel dry.

Passing Clouds

Look up at the sky and notice the clouds. Are they moving fast or floating by slowly?

Pick a cloud that speaks to you and keep your gaze fixed on it. Breathe as you stay connected with that cloud and follow it across the sky. Does it change form? Does it speed up or slow down?

At the end, draw your cloud. Every time you do the exercise, draw another cloud, until the page is filled.

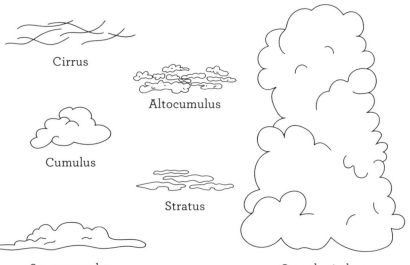

Cirrus

Altocumulus

Cumulus

Stratus

Stratocumulus

Cumulonimbus

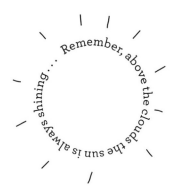

Remember, above the clouds the sun is always shining...

Nature at Work

Research has shown that even a picture of a natural setting has a positive impact on the state of our mind and our ability to focus.

Draw a soothing nature setting into the frame on the right or decorate the frame and use it for a photo of your favorite landscape. Then cut out the page and hang it somewhere in your work space.

Once in a while remember to: Stop. Breathe. Take in the scene.

Flip the page for more ways to find nature at work.

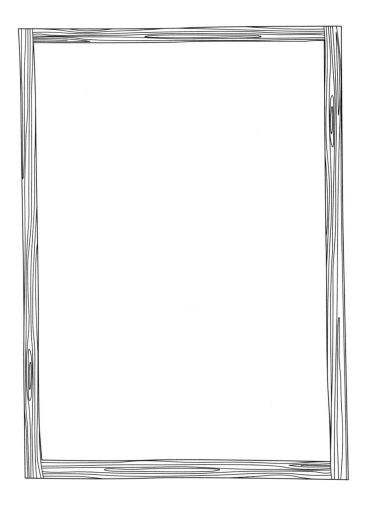

You can find peace anywhere.
Why not right here, now?

**TEN WAYS TO CONNECT WITH
NATURE WHILE ON THE JOB**

- ☑ Hang a photo of your favorite landscape.

- ○ Make your screensaver rotating nature scenes.

- ○ Keep at least one plant on your desk.

- ○ Have lavender or pine-scented oil on hand.

- ○ Open the blinds and/or the windows to let the light and outside in.

- ○ Play nature sounds on your headphones.

- ○ Frame a photo of your pet or favorite animal.

- ○ Take real breaks and go outside (sans phone).

- ○ Listen to your body and the cues it gives you.

- ○ Breathe and take each moment as it comes.

"Ten thousand flowers in spring, the moon in autumn,
a cool breeze in summer, snow in winter.
If your mind isn't clouded by unnecessary things,
this is the best season of your life."

Wu Men Hui-k'ai

Dot to Dot

Slowly connect the dots, moving from each one to the next with each in and out breath.

Ten thousand flowers in spring

A cool breeze in summer

The moon in autumn

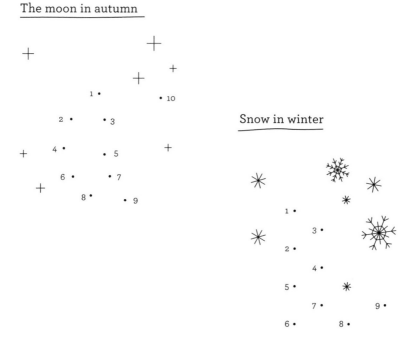

Snow in winter

If your mind isn't clouded by unnecessary things,

1 • 2 • 3 • 4 • 5 •

6 • this is the best
season of your life.

Goethe's Green

Color in the space from the top of the page down to the dotted line below with a sunny yellow.

Color in the space from the bottom of the page up to the wavy line above with an ocean blue.

"The eye experiences a distinctly grateful impression from this color. If the two elementary colors are mixed in perfect equality so that neither predominates, the eye and the mind repose on the result of this junction as upon a simple color. The beholder has neither the wish nor the power to imagine a state beyond it."

Johann Wolfgang von Goethe

Nature's Greens

Fill the squares with other shades of nature's favorite color.
Here are some ideas:

Sea foam

Asparagus

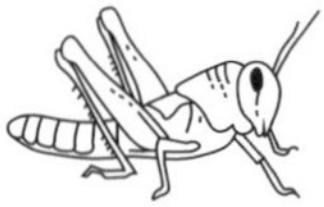

Pistachio

Parakeet

Seaweed

Pine

Gecko

Flower Finder

Flowers come in thousands of different varieties, some unique to where you are. There is no tool to help you find them. You are the flower finder.

Be curious as you go about your day and mindful of all the flowers you can find along the way. See if you can notice at least one in each of the following color categories. Make a sketch and label each flower below.

Yellow

Pink

Dandelion

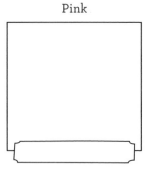

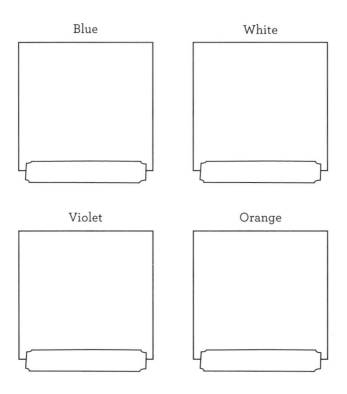

Blue

White

Violet

Orange

"So I will see the tiny purple flowers by the side of the road as I walk to town each day."

Munindraji, as quoted by Tara Brach, on why he meditates

Favorite Animal Profile

What is your favorite animal of all time? Do some detective work and dedicate these pages to them.

Common name:

....

....

Scientific name:

....

....

:= No. 1 =:
FAVORITE
*:= * =:*

Classification: ○ Mammal   ○ Bird   ○ Reptile

                  ○ Amphibian ○ Fish   ○ Insect

Where do they live:

....

How long do they live: Average number of offspring:

.... years

....

Favorite foods:

....

Natural enemies:

....

Relationships: Endangered: Sound it makes:

○ monogamous   ○ yes

○ polygamous   ○ no

○ promiscuous   ○ vulnerable

Other interesting facts you didn't know about your all-time
favorite animal:

....

....

Favorite thing about them:

....

They make me feel:

....

Two other favorite animals in your top three:

✳	✳
✳	✳

Garden of Friends

Choose three friends you really care about. Dedicate a plant or potted flower to each one. It can be a plant you already have, or you can buy one or grow one from a seed (see page 53).

Learn about what each plant needs to thrive and tend to them as you would a friendship.

📷 Share a picture of each honorary plant with your friend. Use the space above, on the pots or on the leaves, to record milestones, fond memories, and tokens of gratitude from your friendship with each person. (If your plant dies, do not worry.)

Purposeful Pests

Earth is home to a huge number of creatures, many wondrous and adorable, others downright frightening or disgusting. Scary spiders and slimy slugs are among the least-favored few.

But what do we actually know about these creepy creatures? See if you can change your sense of worry into wonder by learning more about the work they do in their world.

PEST: Spiders
PURPOSE: *They help control pesky insect populations and their special silk is one of the strongest natural fibers that exists.*

PEST: Slugs
PURPOSE: *They are part of the cleanup crew that works to decompose leaves and plant material back into fertile soil.*

Build your list of least-favorite pests* and a few notes on their purpose.

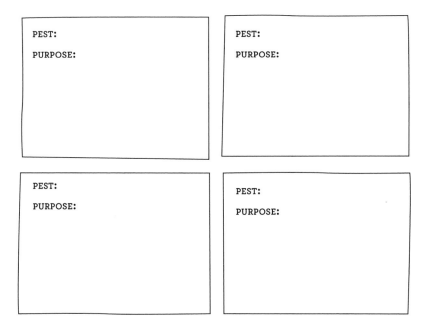

PEST:

PURPOSE:

PEST:

PURPOSE:

PEST:

PURPOSE:

PEST:

PURPOSE:

* Look out for these creatures in real life and spend some time observing them to get to know them.

Leaf Feelings

Plants wear their heart on their leaves – these vital extremities are responsible for a plant's ability to breathe and convert sunlight into energy.

They come in all shapes, sizes, textures, and scents. Each feature serves a special purpose.

Notice in particular how the <u>edges of leaves</u> can vary.

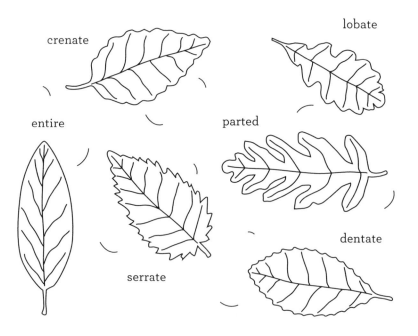

crenate

lobate

entire

parted

serrate

dentate

Feel along the margins and trace their outlines here.

Save your leaves by pressing them between the pages of this book and follow the meditation on the next page.

Leaf Meditation

Close your eyes.

Hold the leaf to your heart and feel as your body breathes. Leaves, too, know how to breathe.

No instructions needed.
Just breathing.

Slowly open your eyes and examine the leaf with a soft gaze. Explore its surface, its veins, its stem, and its edges.
Just seeing.

Carefully take it between your fingers and touch its seams and sense its texture on your fingertips.
Just feeling.

With some gentle pressure, rub your fingers back and forth. Find out if the leaf has a smell.
Just sensing.

Close your eyes again and return to the sense of your body in this moment. With this leaf.
Just being.

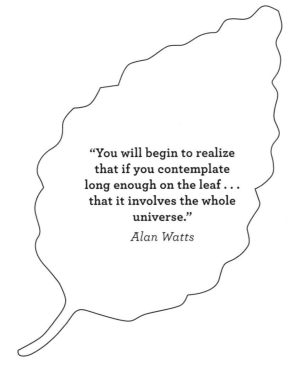

"You will begin to realize
that if you contemplate
long enough on the leaf . . .
that it involves the whole
universe."

Alan Watts

Sensing the Seasons

Every season comes with its sensory delights and dreads. Reflect as you go through the year on what piques your senses. Notice, too, how each experience makes you feel. Hearing, seeing, smelling, touching, tasting . . . feeling. Some ideas are included here. Draw in and label your own.

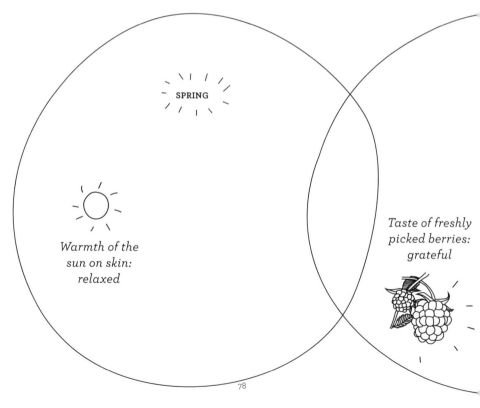

SPRING

Warmth of the sun on skin: relaxed

Taste of freshly picked berries: grateful

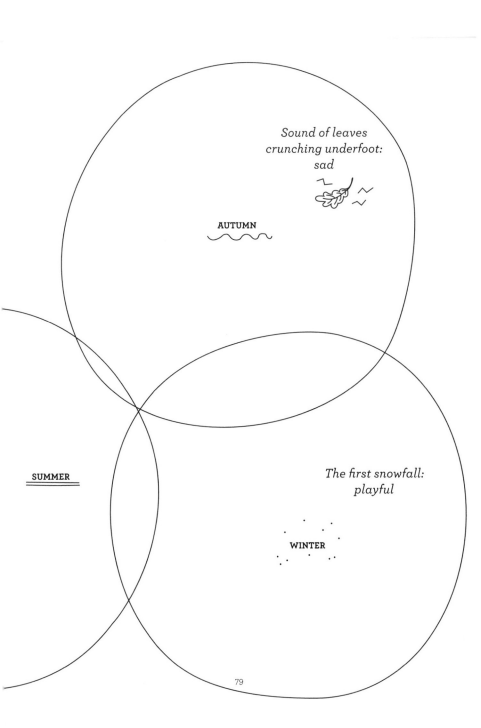

*Sound of leaves
crunching underfoot:
sad*

AUTUMN

SUMMER

*The first snowfall:
playful*

WINTER

Early Bird

On the first Sunday in May, after going to bed early, wake up with the birds. Make yourself a warm cup of tea or coffee and close your eyes as you listen to their orchestra!

Why do birds tend to sing more on spring mornings?

a. The males are declaring their breeding territory.

b. There is nothing else to do in such dim light.

c. To demonstrate their quality as a potential mate.

d. There are fewer other sounds to compete with at that hour.

e. All of the above.

* **EXTRA CREDIT:** Make a thirty-minute recording of this "Dawn Chorus." Listen as needed to soothe your soul.

Breathing Canopy

On a beautiful summer day, lie down beneath a tree. Look up into the canopy of the tree.

As you breathe in, watch one leaf, as you breathe out, move to another leaf.

One breath, one leaf.
Let your attention flow from one leaf to the next.

Your mind may wander off to other things.
Notice where it goes.

To ... a daydream? ... a worry?
... a memory? ... a plan?

Gently come back ...
to breathing with the leaves.

Forest Speak

Go to the woods often and explore the vocabulary of the forest. Find yourself a **smultronställe** where you can sit and practice **dadirri**, while watching the **komorebi** and listening to the **psithurism**. Tick off each word that you get a sense of on your wanderings:

◯ SHINRIN-YOKU *(Japanese)*: The practice of taking in the forest atmosphere or "forest bathing" for its health benefits.

◯ PSITHURISM *(English, from Greek)*: The sound of the wind rustling leaves as it blows through the trees.

◯ SOLIVAGANT *(English, from Latin)*: Wandering alone.

◯ KOMOREBI *(Japanese)*: Sunshine filtering through the leaves of trees as it streams down.

◯ CYNEFIN *(Welsh)*: Habitat – a place where one feels at home and a sense of belonging in the natural environment.

◯ YUGEN *(Japanese)*: A profound awareness of the universe for which there are no words.

◯ TROUVAILLE *(French)*: A lucky find; a chance discovery of something lovely.

◯ PETRICHOR *(English, from Greek)*: The scent of freshly fallen rain on dry earth.

◯ **WALDEINSAMKEIT** *(German)*: The sense of being alone in the woods.

◯ **SMULTRONSTÄLLE** *(Swedish)*: Literally "place of wild strawberries." Used to describe a special and restful hideaway that you love to return to.

◯ **FEUILLEMORT** *(English, from French)*: The color of a fading leaf.

◯ **WABI-SABI** *(Japanese)*: Admiring the beauty of imperfection and embracing the impermanence of nature and life.

◯ **PORONKUSEMA** *(Finnish)*: A measure of distance. How far a reindeer can travel before needing to rest and tinkle. (Max. 4.7 miles.)

◯ **RUDENEJA** *(Lithuanian)*: The feeling of nature in autumn.

◯ **DADIRRI** *(Australian Aboriginal)*: A practice of "deep listening" in stillness and silence to our experience in nature.

◯ **ACATALEPSY** *(English, from Greek)*: The idea that it is impossible to fully comprehend things.

◯ **KAPEL** *(Russian)*: The drip of water as it melts from thawing trees.

◯ **WALDESRAUSCHEN** *(German)*: Sounds of the forest.

Map of Leaves

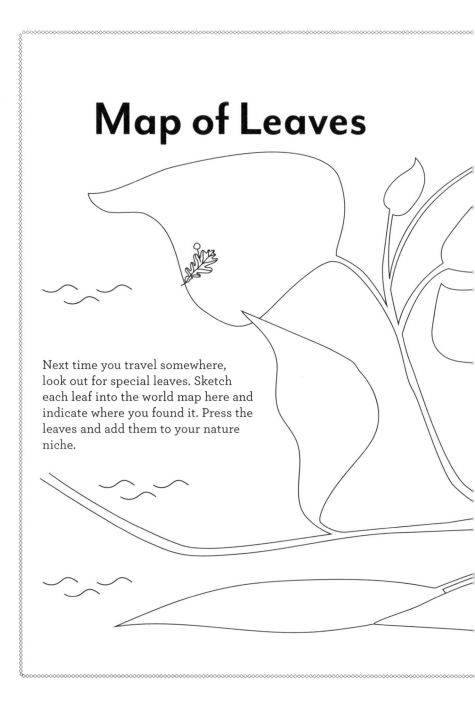

Next time you travel somewhere, look out for special leaves. Sketch each leaf into the world map here and indicate where you found it. Press the leaves and add them to your nature niche.

Flower Gazing

Sit with a flower. Either at home or somewhere outside.

Look into the flower's perfectly symmetrical face. Study this little wonder of nature. Really see it, maybe smell it. Give this flower your full attention.

Simply seeing and being present with the flower   ⟨⋯⋯⋯⋯⋯⋯⋯

Thoughts about the flower   ⟨⋯⋯⋯⋯⋯⋯⋯⋯

Thoughts about other things, places, and times   ⟨⋯⋯⋯⋯⋯⋯

Notice where your mind goes when it wanders off.

Then gently bring it back to taking in the flower.

Bark Rubbing

Each tree's unique bark is like its fingerprint. Use a pencil or crayon to capture the impression of a few tree trunks here.

Hold the page over the bark and rub with enough pressure to pick up the pattern. See if you can match them to different categories of bark, shown below:

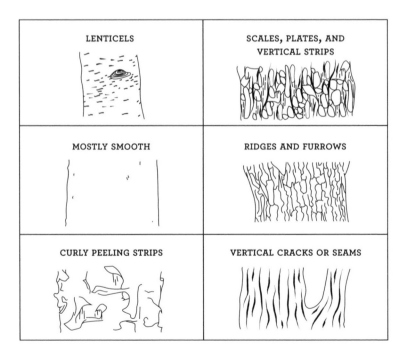

"The greatest wonder is that we can see these trees and not wonder more."

Ralph Waldo Emerson

Into the Woods

Make your way to a forest. Find a place to sit
for a while. Make a square yard yours and stay
for one . . . maybe two . . . sometimes three hours.

There is nothing to do. Just be.

No need to meditate.

> **"I felt in need of a great pilgrimage so I sat still . . . "**
>
> *Abu Hajiz Kabir*

Just be curious. Notice nature. Observe your inner world. Be with the whole of your experience.

Stay warm. Stay hydrated. Stay awake.

Surf the urges to leave
(unless you're in real trouble).

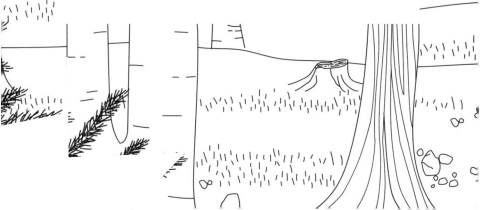

Congrats! Note any insights gained here.

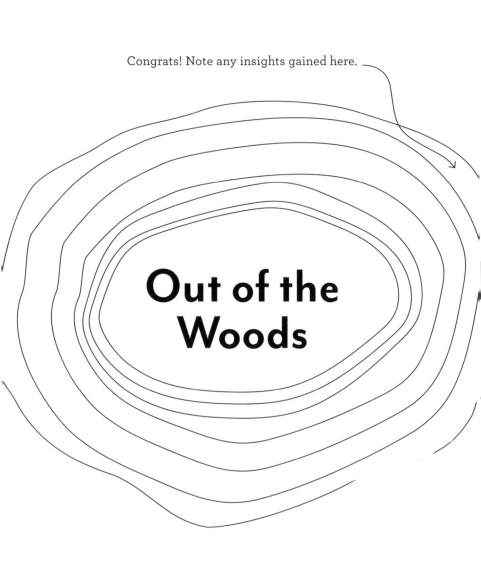

Out of the Woods

Animal Meditation

Close your eyes and bring to mind your favorite animal. Imagine it standing in front of you, looking back at you. Feel the presence of your animal.

Notice how being with your animal makes you feel inside. Happy, calm, excited? Stay with this feeling. Enjoy it.

If it feels right, reach out to the animal and feel its fur or skin. Maybe even lean against it or cuddle it.

Stay with your animal as long as you like. Enjoy its presence.

. . . and once you are ready, open your eyes.

Letting Go

Falling leaves in autumn are the perfect metaphor for letting go. But it is not by force or sheer will of the tree that its leaves are shed. They fall as nature takes its course. Each leaf in its own time.

"It's not a matter of letting go – you would if you could. Instead of *Let it go* we should probably say *Let it be*."

Jon Kabat-Zinn

Sense the season's same grace and fill the illustrated leaves to represent the things in your life that you intend to set free and let be.

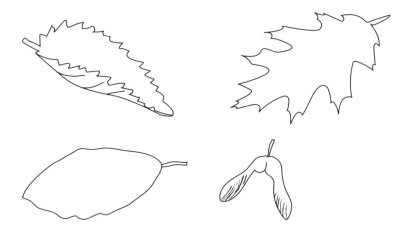

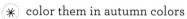 color them in autumn colors

Vitamin Sea

In bygone eras, doctors prescribed seaside stays to treat all kinds of physical and mental ailments. It was thought that both the salt air and water had healing properties. Here is your prescription for some sensory seaside therapy.

Name:

_____

R℞

SEASIDE THERAPY

Directions

— 3 x dunks in the ocean water
— 1 x seaside sunrise or sunset
— 5 reps x 3 mindful breaths of seaside air
— 1 x lathering of sunscreen (reapply as needed)
— 1 x barefoot stroll in the sand
— 1 x building a sandcastle

Rest for a while and read the poem "Let It Go" by Danna Faulds.

✳ In tropical settings, a snorkeling excursion is highly advisable to enhance the mindful enjoyment and therapeutic benefits.

Sea creatures seen:

Sounds heard:

Beachcomber finds:

Wonders witnessed:

Insights gained:

One Summer's Day

There is a lush green lawn waiting for you. Go there and lie down in the grass under the big sky. Watch the clouds float by. Look in between the blades of grass. Listen to the birds and the wind in the trees.

Are you there yet?

Who made the world?
Who made the swan, and the black bear?
Who made the grasshopper?
This grasshopper, I mean –
the one who has flung herself out of the grass,
the one who is eating sugar out of my hand,
who is moving her jaws back and forth instead of up and down –
who is gazing around with her enormous and complicated eyes.
Now she lifts her pale forearms and thoroughly washes her face.
Now she snaps her wings open, and floats away.
I don't know exactly what a prayer is.
I do know how to pay attention, how to fall down
into the grass, how to kneel down in the grass,
how to be idle and blessed, how to stroll through the fields,
which is what I have been doing all day.
Tell me, what else should I have done?
Doesn't everything die at last, and too soon?
<u>Tell me, what is it you plan to do</u>
<u>with your one wild and precious life?</u>

Mary Oliver, "The Summer Day"

1901

"Thousands of tired, nerve-shaken, over-civilized people are beginning to find out that going to the mountains is going home; that wildness is a necessity; and that mountain parks and reservations are useful not only as fountains of timber and irrigating rivers, but as fountains of life."

John Muir (circa 1901)

Make a list of national parks that you would like to visit (in your own country or abroad):

○ ....
○ ....
○ ....
○ ....
○ ....
○ ....
○ ....
○ ....
○ ....
○ ....
○ ....
○ ....

Make plans. Tick them off as you go.

Backtrack

Go on a walk through the park or woods with a good friend. On your way, talk and use your phones as needed.

At some point, turn around and go back the way you came. This time, walk together in silence and keep your phones off.

Friend's name: ....

Discuss your experience together.

Was the way back different?

Yes ◯

No ◯

If yes, how?

....

....

....

....

....

....

....

....

....

Blind Bouquet

Grab a pencil and draw a bouquet of flowers from memory with your eyes closed. No peeking! Just wait for it . . . unleash your inner artist.

×

Place pencil here to start

Second try here:

And now, color in your drawings – eyes open.

Starry Night

On a clear summer night, sit still and watch the sky. As time passes, more and more stars will appear and the universe will reveal itself to you.

✳ Draw as many stars here as you can count. Watch for falling stars.

o

North
Star

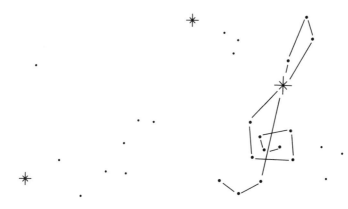

Now rest. And listen to this night-sky playlist:

"Across the Universe," The Beatles

"Moonlight Sonata," Beethoven

"Stand by Me," Ben E. King

"Nocturne, Op. 9, No. 2," Chopin

"Moondance," Van Morrison

"Somewhere Out There," Phillip Glasser and Betsy Cathcart, from
the movie *An American Tail: Fievel Goes West*

Life of a Tree

From their roots to their crown and their shade all around, trees are silently spectacular. <u>Find yourself a tree to admire</u>. Sit down and lean up against its trunk as you contemplate all the ways that it is working.

(1) Every single leaf springs from a bud after a sleepy season of waiting for its cues – longer days, more rain, warmer air.

(2) Raindrops trickle through the trees in search of soil.

(3) Rocks in the soil give off minerals.

(4) Roots anchored deep and wide reach for water and minerals.

(5) The trunk holds it all together, housing the highways for water and nutrients to flow. Up and out the tree will grow.

(6) Water, air, and sunlight unite amid the green goodness of thousands of leaves. Together they create food for the tree and set pure oxygen free.

7 Birds nest high in the treetops, safe from their foes. Foraging and feasting on the tree-loving pests. Some fly farther afield, unknowingly sowing the seeds of their tree.

8 As autumn approaches, leaves will lose their luster and flutter to the ground. This leafy litter protects the soil from being washed away.

9 Animals that are grateful for shade, shelter, and snacks return fertilizer to the surrounding soil.

10 Under the surface, mini microbes and crawly creatures are hard at work, breaking down old leaf litter and churning the soil.

On it goes . . . recycling nature's nutrients. And with each new year another ring is marked within its ancient trunk.

Go Out and Play

Children interact with nature in such fun and playful ways. We can do that, too. Tick all the activities you want to do from the list below and add your own. Then, do them!

○ Walk through autumn leaves

○ Wear cherries as earrings

○ String grapes as a necklace

○ Build a snowman

○ Make a snow angel

○ Catch
s
n
o
w
f
l
a
k
e
s
on your tongue

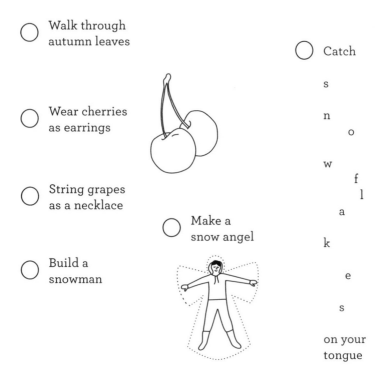

○ Whistle through
a blade of grass

○ Climb a tree
(at your own risk!)

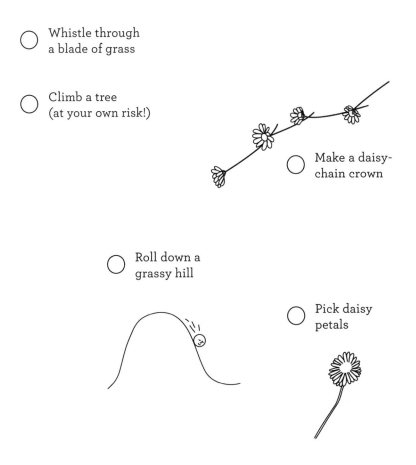

○ Make a daisy-
chain crown

○ Roll down a
grassy hill

○ Pick daisy
petals

✳ ✳ ✳ *Stay curious* ✳ ✳ ✳

Deep Blue Sea

The ocean is home to some fascinating animals and plants. Color in the sea-life scene below. Look up the featured creatures and choose your colors accordingly.

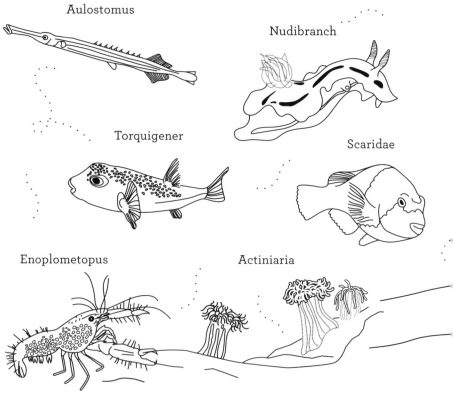

Aulostomus

Nudibranch

Torquigener

Scaridae

Enoplometopus

Actiniaria

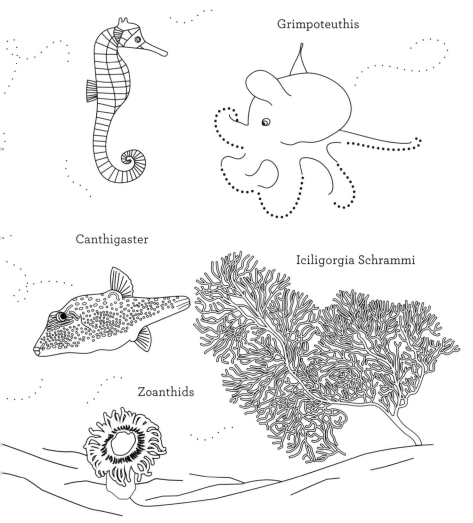

Hippocampus

Grimpoteuthis

Canthigaster

Iciligorgia Schrammi

Zoanthids

. . . dive deeper and find out how they spend their days.

Healing Herb Garden

Cultivate your own herb garden – indoors or out. Not only can they spice up your meals, but herbs actually have some potent medicinal properties. Do some research and note their uses below for your own herbal apothecary.

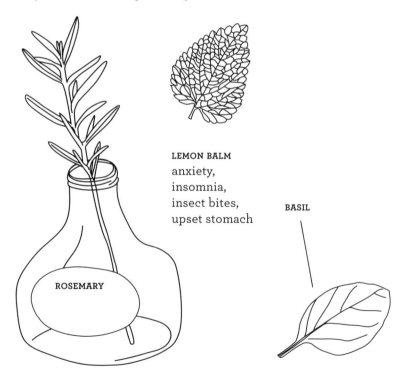

LEMON BALM
anxiety,
insomnia,
insect bites,
upset stomach

BASIL

ROSEMARY

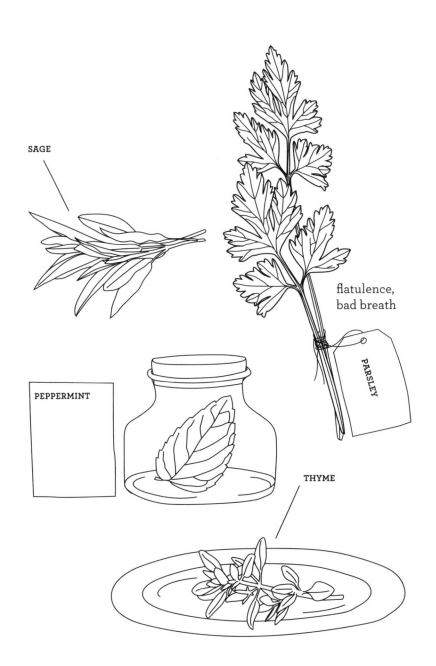

SAGE

flatulence,
bad breath

PARSLEY

PEPPERMINT

THYME

Mountain Meditation

The imagery of a mountain can evoke qualities worth cultivating. Strength, balance, quiet confidence . . . see what a mountain evokes in you. Follow each instruction one by one. Always return to your breath and body as you sense the mountain's qualities.

Imagine it enduring all sorts of weather . . . strong winds sweeping through, pelting rain, and even snow. Imagine it as winter gives way to spring . . . summer to autumn.

Close your eyes. Imagine your mountain in the distance. Picture it at different times of day . . . sunrise and sunset . . . in the moonlight.

**START
HERE**

Sit with your back upright and your body tall . . . become your mountain. Find your base through the breath.

Through all of this, the mountain stands tall, at ease with whatever each moment brings and enjoying the ordinary – a flower blooming, warm sunshine on a spring day, happy goats roaming the summer mountainside.

See if you can embody the same ease of being. Feel grounded in each moment, breathing with whatever comes up, knowing that bad weather passes and seasons change. But you can be a mountain still.

> **"The birds have vanished into the sky, and now the last cloud drains away. We sit together, the mountain and me, until only the mountain remains."**
>
> *Li Po*
> *(Translated by Sam Hamill)*

Color in and decorate your mountain as you like.

Fresh Air Challenge

For fifteen days, take an extra fifteen minutes beyond your normal routine to enjoy being outdoors in the fresh air. Make an X below each time you take your legs for a stretch or stroll.

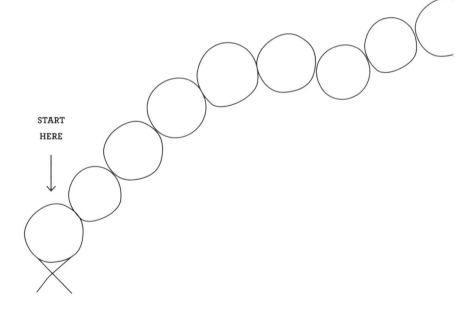

START
HERE

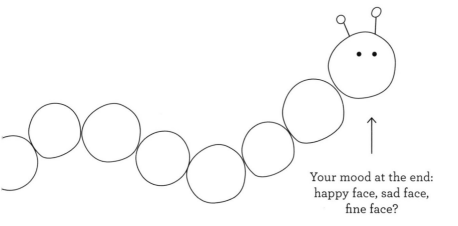

Your mood at the end:
happy face, sad face,
fine face?

Fresh Flower Challenge

For one month, make sure to always have a fresh flower somewhere in your favorite room. Greet it in the morning and in the evening, until it has faded.

Sketch your favorite flowers into the vases below to preserve their memory.

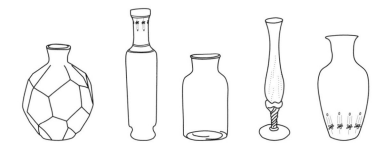

Before you throw them away, share with them these parting words:

> Thanks for brightening my days.
> Now, it's time to say goodbye.
> Farewell, and many happy returns.
> It was a joy to have you.

Land-escapes

Reflect on all the feelings, findings, experiences, and past and future destinations that these landscape features evoke. Note your associations around each one below.

FOREST

VALLEY

RIVER

CREEK

LAKE

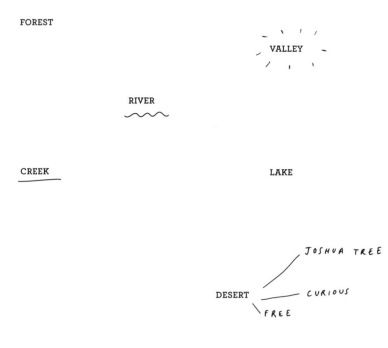

JOSHUA TREE

DESERT — CURIOUS

FREE

WATERFALL

MOUNTAIN

MEADOW

HILL

OCEAN

POND

Spend some time at/in/on _____ . Update your sense of the place.

My favorite landscape is _____ .

Point of View

A mountain peak, hilltop, or vista point – find yourself a place with perspective. Rest here for a while. Breathe with the wind.

The beauty of the trees,
the softness of the air,
the fragrance of the grass,
speaks to me.
The summit of the mountain,
the thunder of the sky,
the rhythm of the sea,
speaks to me.
The faintness of the stars,
the freshness of the morning,
the dew drop on the flower,
speaks to me.
The strength of fire,
the taste of salmon,
the trail of the sun,
And the life that never goes away,
They speak to me.
And my heart soars.

Chief Dan George

REFLECTION

One lofty life goal:

....

One whimsical wish:

....

A sense of this moment to remember:

....

....

....

....

....

....

....

Night Wander

On a full moon, go out for a night walk. Pay attention to the different shades of darkness. Once in a while, become still, and extinguish your flashlight. As your eyes adjust to the darkness, you will see more and more.

In the darkness . . .

. . . listen, like a fox

. . . smell, like a dog

. . . feel, like a cat's whiskers

. . . look, like an owl

"I could see every pebble on the path, and every blade of grass, by that splendid moon."

Emily Brontë

Staycation Collage

Create a collage to inspire you and remind you of the nature
you most love.

Magazine clippings of nature scenes, trees, leaves, flowers,
patterns, or words that capture the essence of how nature feels . . .
cut them out and glue them in here.

Add your own photographs, mementos, or found objects, too.

Fill to the edge of the page.

Fill to the edge of the page.

When you can't get away, come here for a nature staycation.
Breathe, see, sense, and soften.

Nature's Gift Shop

Here are some ideas for easy-to-make or gather gifts for family and friends:

Lavender bags
Potpourri
Birdseed feeder
Seedling or plant
Framed dried leaves
Seeds to plant
Fresh fruit basket
Sea shells
Special stones
Pressed flower or leaf greeting card
Wildflower bouquet
Pickings for a tea infusion
Dried flowers

Sea salt and honey face mask

Picture frame from twigs

Gift voucher for a walk or picnic together

A poem you wrote about nature

Your artwork from pages 108 to 109

Your own granola mix

Sand from your beach vacation

Photos from your nature excursions

A contact-paper bookmark with a pressed flower

"All good things are wild and free."

Henry David Thoreau

Secret Seed

Pine cones hold the seeds to their trees. With some patience and care, you can harvest these seeds and grow a tiny tree.

(1) In the late-summer or early-autumn months, go to a forest with plenty of pines.

(2) Collect pine cones that have not yet fully opened – gather as many as you can. Those fresh from the tree will need to be kept in a warm place or laid in the sun to help them open.

(3) Once open, you can hit the top of the cone against a hard surface to shake out the seeds.

(4) To find which of these winged wonders are most likely to germinate, put them in water overnight (remove the wings first). Those that sink are the best candidates.

(5) These winners will still need their winter, so place them in a plastic baggie with a damp paper towel and keep them in the refrigerator for thirty to fifty days.

(6) The seeds will then be ready to sow. Plant each one each in a small pot of damp soil and keep in a sunny spot. Water daily.

(7) Look for signs of life within a couple weeks. Once any of your seedlings grow to about six inches tall, they are ready to be replanted.

⑧ Return to the woods where you found your pine cones and choose a special place to plant one of your seedlings.

⑨ Mark it with a ring of rocks or anchor a stick in the ground nearby. Return here sometimes, to see how it is doing.

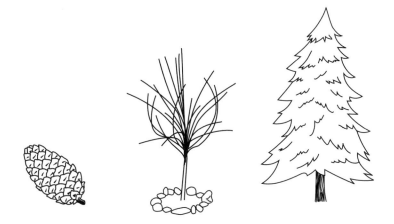

p.s. If there are no pines in your neck of the woods, do some research and try this with another type of forest tree or plant.

Your Square Yard

Find a place to sit in the wild. Either on a patch of grass or an earthy surface. Explore the square yard around you. Look under rocks, turn over leaves, dig in the soil, peek into the grass, notice all the micro movements . . .

When you have finished exploring, sit for a while and contemplate the cubic yard of earth beneath you.

There is a whole system of exchanges here that brings nutrients to life. In just a handful of topsoil, there are more microorganisms than people on Earth.

Flower Press

Go on a walk and look for wildflowers along the way. Collect them, and press them in this or another book overnight.

Once they are dry, glue them onto these pages. Add as many flowery friends as you like. Savor the beauty and the feelings of awe that arise when you return to your piece of wild art.

TIP: Cover each side of the page with a piece of wax paper to protect your flowers. Use extra pressed flowers to make wild greeting cards.

Weather Walks

Don't just watch the weather from your window. Go out and connect with all the ways it makes you feel.

RAINY DAY WANDER: Pitter-patter of rain on the umbrella. Wearing rain boots to splash around. Grateful for raindrops on rooftops and windows.

SPRING SUNSHINE SAUNTER: Take a walk through the park. Flowers sprouting up all around. The smell of wet ground. First buds on trees. Yippee!

SNOW DRIFTING: Fluffy snow suspended in the trees. Frozen clusters crunching underfoot. Foggy breath hovering in the air. Warmly dressed and well prepared . . . making the cold easier to bear.

BLUSTERY/WINDY WALK: Hair blowing everywhere . . . don't care. Safe inside a warm jacket. Stinging cheeks. Breathing with and not resisting the wind.

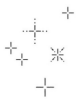

COOL SUMMER NIGHT STROLL: Moonlight echoing across the fields. Sweet breeze relieving the heat. Feeling free and happy to be.

HAILSTORM HURRY:

OTHER WEATHER MUSINGS:

Like the weather . . .
"Just keep going. No feeling is final."
Rainer Maria Rilke

Scents of Nature

Nature is full of scents to savor – not just the lavender, roses, and freshly cut grass in spring. Start exploring the smells of the leaves, bark, wood, the earth, fields, herbs . . . even the muddy pond.

Rub objects on this
page to capture scents.

ATTENTION! Your senses are the gateway to the present moment.
When you get lost in thought, grab a piece of nature, close your
eyes, and come back to presence through your sense of smell.

Wonder-full Windows

Connect with nature right outside your window, whether at home or on the go. Look at the scenes that you can observe from afar, maybe as a passenger in a car, or from a plane, or on a train. Look at the sunlight and the shadows, the textures and the colors, trees blowing in the wind, clouds sailing by, animals resting in the fields. Take in all the wonders from right where you are.

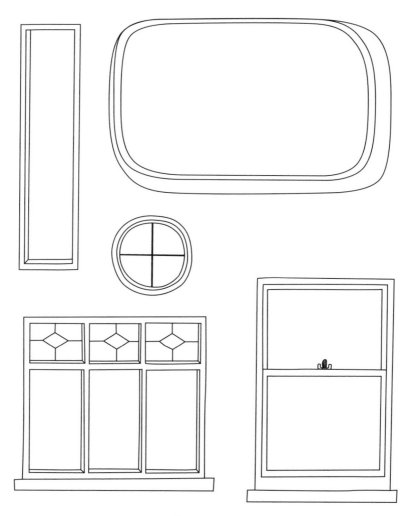

Sketch in your most memorable views.

Thank You Notes to Nature

Nature offers so much to be grateful for. Notice each time you sense a feeling of gratitude for one of nature's wonders, and draft a thank you note here.

Dear sheep who gave its wool for my favorite winter sweater, thank you for all the joy and warmth!

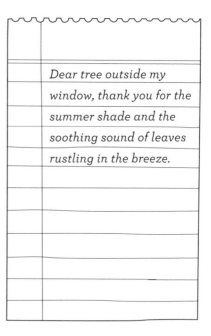

Dear tree outside my window, thank you for the summer shade and the soothing sound of leaves rustling in the breeze.

Take Time

Take this sundial with you into nature. Use it to track the motion and miracle of time as you explore or rest.

HOW TO USE IT:

(1) Insert a recycled "bendy straw" into the center of the sundial, bendy side down, tucked underneath the back of the page.

(2) Rotate the book until the straw is pointing due north.

(3) The face should be pitched upward – adjust the angle to bring the dial into line with the current time.

NOTE: The sundial is designed for summer time (daylight saving time) in the northern hemisphere. It can also work in winter – test it out to see how.

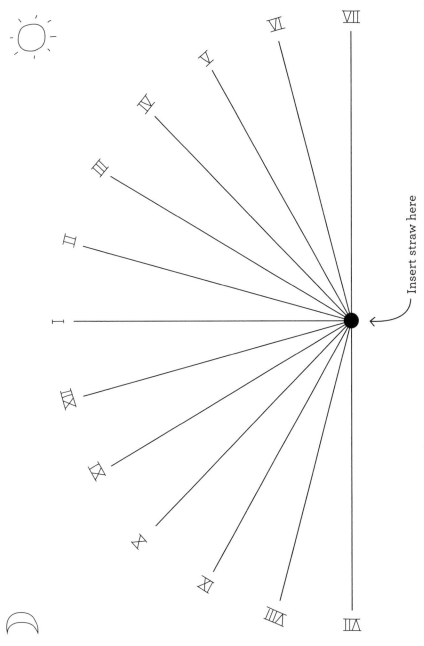

Insert straw here

Inner and Outer Space

Practice expanding your awareness from your breath to your whole body to imagining and sensing all the space around you. Close your eyes as you sense and imagine . . .

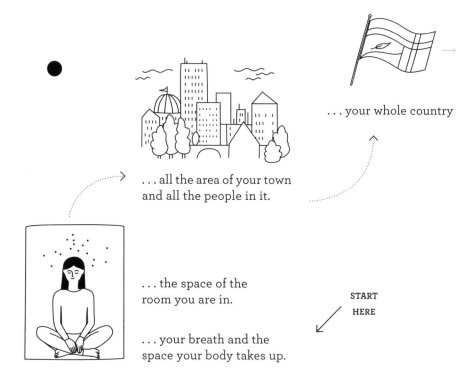

. . . your whole country

. . . all the area of your town and all the people in it.

. . . the space of the room you are in.

START HERE

. . . your breath and the space your body takes up.

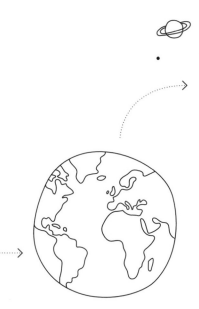

. . . this beautiful planet, amid a
universe of endless space and stars.

. . . the whole wide world and
everyone in it.

. . . return to your own body, breathing right
here, in this moment, held in all this space.

Hello Wild Thing

The human body is one of the most amazing works of nature around. Here are some ways to tune in to the aliveness of the living organism that is your own body.

Place one hand on your belly and close your eyes while you tune in to the sensations of your breath.

Hold your hands out in your lap, either palms up or clasped together. Focus your attention on the sensations around and inside your hands.

When you are out and about, use your feet as a gateway to come back to the present moment. Drop in and feel your feet on the ground and how they move and carry you with each step.

Sit down and close your eyes. Notice all the little colored shapes that sprinkle up behind your closed eyelids. Then gently open your eyes and let the light come in. Look around. Remember what a wonder it is that we can see!

Sit still and feel your heart beating in your chest or through your pulse, one heartbeat at a time. Then get up, walk around at a fast pace, and then sit down again. Feel how your heart beats faster now. Your body is working all day!

Awesome Facts

Growing our knowledge of nature can be another way of inspiring a sense of awe. Add more nuggets of knowledge to the list of awesome facts below.

✳ The average human body contains more than 60,000 miles (97,000 km) worth of blood vessels.

→ Sea otters have a skin flap where they store their favorite rock, which they use to open shells.

→ Whales and goats can have regional "accents."

✳ A Japanese koi fish once lived for 226 years.

"Hello again, Daphne!"

✳ Crows can recognize faces and mimic human voices.

→ The smell of freshly cut grass is actually a distress call to beckon certain insects.

→ Cows can have a best friend and show signs of distress when separated from them.

 Dust blown over from the Sahara Desert helps fertilize the Amazon rainforest.

✳

→

✳

✳

→

Sensory Salad

Buy the following veggies at your local store: celery, carrots, cucumbers, and tomatoes. Cut them into rounds and admire their internal symmetry.

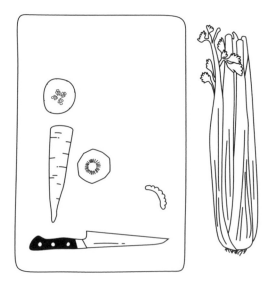

Draw them here. And as you do so, notice their textures and scents.

When done, gently place everything into a salad bowl. Dress with vinegar, oil, and seasoning to taste . . . then savor your salad mindfully. :)

Life Lessons

Nature reveals great wisdom – if we only pause and listen. Read the life lessons below out loud.

THE SKY SAYS:
Stay open to what arises. Tomorrow always brings a new day.

THE TREE SAYS:
Bend with the wind. Learn to let go. Trust your strength.

THE FLOWER SAYS:
Bloom where you are planted. Reach for what nourishes you.

THE OCEAN SAYS:
Storms always pass. Don't fight the current.

THE STREAM SAYS:
Go with the flow. Get around creatively. The path will reveal itself.

THE STONE SAYS:
Wherever I go, there I am.

#IntoNature

Cut out and color the following reminder. Put it in your wallet, on your desk, or by your bed. Take it on your walks and take pictures of beautiful nature scenes with it in the foreground. Share the photos of your mindful nature moments with others. #IntoNature

Be right back . . . gone <u>into nature.</u>

Magnify-cent

Get a magnifying glass or a pair of binoculars and start exploring nature up close.

Tree Forms

Different types of trees have different growth habits. Over the next weeks, whenever you are outside and encounter trees, look out for the different shapes – use the illustrations below as a guide. Once you've found a tree form illustrated below, color in the respective tree.

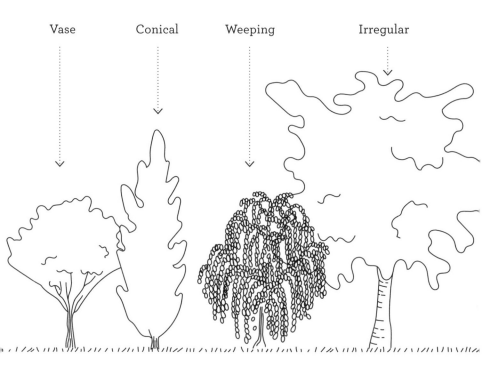

Vase   Conical   Weeping   Irregular

Open   Fountain   Oval   Pyramidal   Spreading

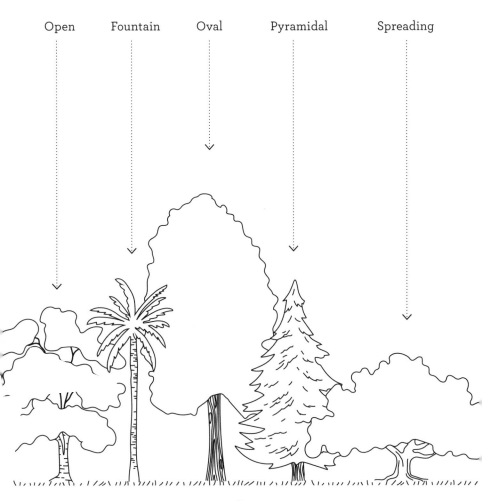

Wild Supermarket

The term *foraging* means the act of gathering food (edible plants, flowers, and fungi) in the wild. Foraging in the woods and fields was once a way of life. Go out into nature's wild supermarket and gather some goods yourself.

Here are some examples. Add your local finds.

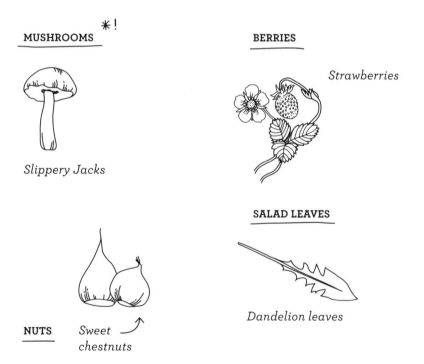

MUSHROOMS ＊!

Slippery Jacks

BERRIES

Strawberries

SALAD LEAVES

Dandelion leaves

NUTS *Sweet chestnuts*

EDIBLE FLOWERS

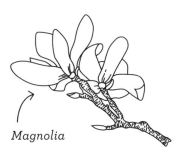

Magnolia

WILD HERBS

Wild garlic

TEA OR TINCTURE LEAVES

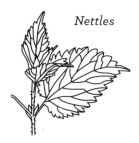

Nettles

✳! CAUTION: Make sure you know what you're picking, as some things look delicious but may be deadly.

Spelling Stones

The earth generates amazing rocks and gemstones – some of nature's most precious treasures. In Victorian times, the first letters of certain gemstones were used to spell out secret messages in rings and other jewels.

Look at this list of gemstones, where the first letters of each stone spell out the word *nature*. Then color in the shapes with the correct gemstone color.

N   irvana quartz

A   methyst

T   urquoise

U   vite

R   uby

E   merald

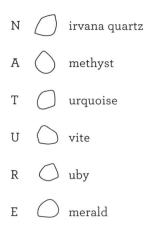

"I believe in God, only I spell it Nature."
Frank Lloyd Wright

Look up acrostic gemstones and spell out other messages according to the gemstone colors here (add more as needed):

Play Your Part

The more we get to know nature, the clearer it becomes that everything is interconnected. Our planet hangs in a delicate balance, and small changes to our lifestyles can have cascading effects elsewhere in the supply/food chain.

Get informed. Find a cause. Do your part.

Here is a list of documentaries to get you started:

- *Oceans*
- *An Inconvenient Truth*
- *Bambi*
- *Mission Blue*
- *The True Cost*
- *Food, Inc.*
- *The Story of Stuff*
- *Cowspiracy*
- *Trashed*
- *The Cove*
- *Earthlings*
- *In Pursuit of Silence*
- *How to Let Go of the World and Love All the Things Climate Can't Change*

What can you do to make a difference?

Example:

ISSUE:
There are garbage vortexes in our oceans, some more than 300,000 square miles in size. The plastic is harming sea life and birds.

MY PART:
Use less plastic. Recycle. Donate to the Ocean Cleanup fund.

ISSUE: ....
....
....

YOUR PART: ....
....
....
....
....
....

YOUR CAUSE:

Animal Connection

Animals are a central part of nature and they live all around us – both in the countryside and in cities. Try these ways of connecting with them and see how it can enrich your life:

- Notice an ant and watch it for a while.
- Feed a sparrow in the park.
- Track down a spider in your home and set it free.
- Admire a swan or different duck species in your park.
- Visit a farm and greet the pigs, chickens, donkeys, and sheep.
- Offer dog-walking or pet-sitting services.
- Get to know your neighborhood cats.
- Visit an animal sanctuary or shelter.
- Pet a dog in the street.
- Hang a birdfeeder outside your window.
- Grow a butterfly.

VIRTUAL WAYS TO CONNECT:

— Watch nature documentaries: *Terra, Planet Earth, Life.*

— Subscribe to the Dodo or other animal video sites.

— Follow famous pets (e.g., My Best Friend Hank or Norbert) on Facebook.

— Download a cat-purring app (e.g., Purrli).

— Visit museums or art exhibitions featuring animals.

— Subscribe to a nature magazine like *National Geographic.*

Happy Campfire

There is something magical about fire. This force that just ignites out of thin air has sustained countless lives and livelihoods over time.

Here is a list of some of the things you need for building a campfire yourself:

1. **TINDER:** Dry grass, paper, birch tree bark, cotton balls. Don't pack too tightly.

2. **KINDLING:** Small sticks and twigs, dry leaves, cedar bark. Arrange at an angle up around the tinder.

3. **FIRE STARTER OPTIONS:**

   ✕ Matches   ✕ Magnifying glass
   ✕ Fire plough   ✕ Flint and steel striker
   ✕ Hand drill

4. **FUEL WOOD:** Larger dry logs and chopped wood. Start small. Fire needs to breathe.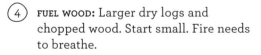

Gather your friends and get out your guitar. Or follow the fire meditation instructions on page 176.

✳! CAUTION: Check the fire safety rules of your location before you start.

Fire Meditation

FEEL:
Feel the warmth the fire gives off. Feel it on your cheeks, your hands, and the rest of your body. Mindfully move closer to it, and then farther away.

SMELL:
Pay attention to the smell of the fire. For a couple of moments, even smell the smoke and let it get on your clothes to capture the smell for the next day.

LISTEN:
Notice the sounds of the fire. The crackling. The sound of logs shifting as they burn down.

SEE:
Look into the fire. Study the colors . . . of the burning coal, the flames dancing. Pay attention to how the fire constantly changes.

TASTE:
Roast a marshmallow over the fire.
Then eat it.

What feelings does the fire evoke? Nostalgia, gratitude, memories, dreams ... Use the spaces below to note what comes to mind. Surrender each piece to the fire.

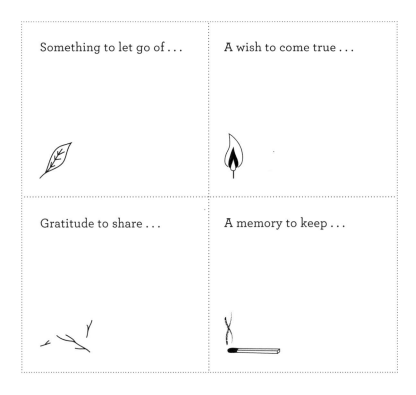

Something to let go of ...

A wish to come true ...

Gratitude to share ...

A memory to keep ...

Field Journal

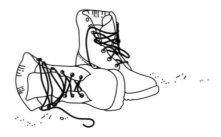

Field Notes

In addition to completing the specific exercises in this book, take time to regularly explore the great outdoors. Really IMMERSE yourself in nature.

You do not have to go far or anywhere at all. Whether on a walk in the park, a hike in the hills, or just sitting by a stream or lying under a tree, you can be mindful and feel inspired.

Here are some tips for ways to explore and connect:

○ MINDFULLY EXPLORE: Apply the Mindful Wandering steps in different locations/routes. Remember "Permission, Intention, Attention, and Attitude" are key (see page 22).

○ WALK SLOWLY: Practice mindful walking. Sense your feet on the ground with each step, and tether your attention between your inner and outer worlds. Play with your pace – see how it feels to walk at half of your normal speed. Then go even slower.

○ SIT FOR A WHILE: You don't always need to move. You can also just find a place to sit or lay down. Sense the space around you. Use your senses to explore your surroundings from right where you are.

The field notes pages that follow are designed for you to document your explorations and experiences. (Photocopy blank templates for an ongoing supply.)

"I go to nature to be soothed and healed, and to have my senses put in order."

John Burroughs

Go well, mindful wanderer!
May you find peace of mind and a sense of connection in nature . . .

Field Notes

(EXAMPLE)

DATA POINTS

Departure date/time:
OCTOBER 22 17:00

Return date/time:
OCTOBER 22 18:00

Route/destination:
STATE PARK.
LOOPING AROUND THE
LAKE, UP AND AROUND
LOOKOUT PEAK, AND
ENDING BACK AT THE
START.

Terrain and features (river, sea, woods, etc.):
FOLLOWED PUBLIC FOOTPATH
ALONG THE LAKE TO BASE OF
THE HILL. UNDULATING TERRAIN
TO START, BEFORE STEEP
ASCENT TOWARD THE TOP.
STOPPED BY LARGE GROUP OF
ROCKS. VIEW OF THE LAKE AND
RIVER TO THE EAST. QUITE
STEEP HILL AT THE END.

Distance covered:
7.7 MILES

Avg. tempo: 0

1   3
        6
  2
5   7 (4)   9
    8
        10

External weather

Internal weather

CRISP AIR,
CLEAR SKIES,
LIGHT
BREEZE.

NERVOUS ABOUT NEW
ROUTE. PLAYFUL
ON ROCKS, PROUD AT
PEAK.

DISCOVERIES

Sights:
EXPANSIVE VIEWS IN ALL
DIRECTIONS. MOON RISING
TOWARD EVENING.

Sounds: FAMILIES LAUGHING / TALKING ON THE TRAIL. SCURRYING LIZARDS.

Smells:
WOODLAND PINES!
BBQ. DAMP GRASS.

Sensations: COOLNESS OF EVENING. STRAIN ON LEGS GOING UP / DOWN HILL.

Takeaway treasures:
- GREY FEATHER
- PINECONE FROM FOREST

Wildlife spotting:
SQUIRRELS! LOTS OF
HUMANS, BIRDS, LIZARDS.

Notes/sketches:

WARM HANDS, COOL CHEEKS.

KESTREL
SPOTTED
ON POST

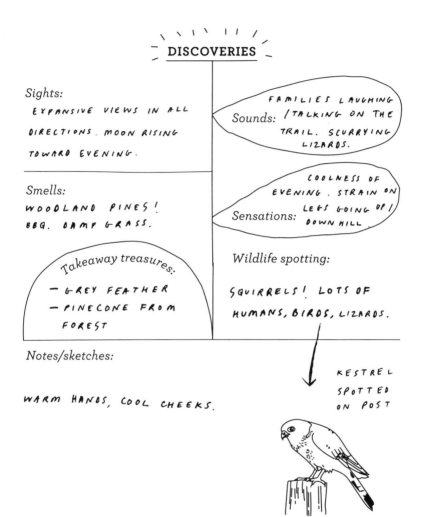

Gratitude and insights:

COOLER AUTUMN DAYS DON'T HAVE TO KEEP ME INDOORS.

GRATEFUL FOR PEAKS AND PERSPECTIVE.

Field Notes

DATA POINTS

Departure date/time: *Return date/time:*

Route/destination: *Terrain and features (river, sea, woods, etc.):*

Distance covered:

Avg. tempo: 0   *External weather*

1   3   *Internal weather*
              6
     2
5   7   4   9
        8
              10

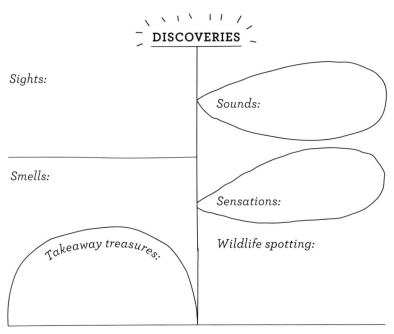

DISCOVERIES

Sights:

Sounds:

Smells:

Sensations:

Takeaway treasures:

Wildlife spotting:

Notes/sketches:

Gratitude and insights:

Field Notes

DATA POINTS

Departure date/time: *Return date/time:*

Route/destination: *Terrain and features (river, sea, woods, etc.):*

Distance covered:

Avg. tempo: 0   *External weather*

1   3   *Internal weather*
                6
     2
5   7   4   9

        8
                10

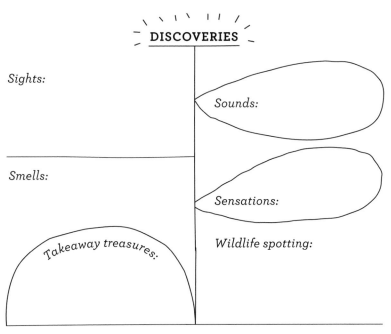

DISCOVERIES

Sights:

Sounds:

Smells:

Sensations:

Takeaway treasures:

Wildlife spotting:

Notes/sketches:

Gratitude and insights:

_____

_____

Field Notes

DATA POINTS

Departure date/time: | *Return date/time:*

Route/destination: | *Terrain and features (river, sea, woods, etc.):*

Distance covered:

Avg. tempo:

0

1   3

6

2

5   7   4   9

8

10

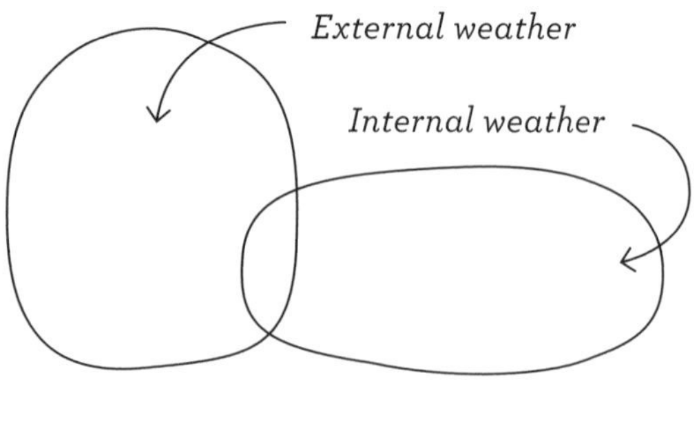

External weather

Internal weather

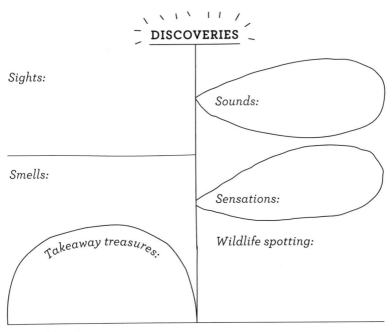

DISCOVERIES

Sights:

Sounds:

Smells:

Sensations:

Takeaway treasures:

Wildlife spotting:

Notes/sketches:

Gratitude and insights:

Field Notes

DATA POINTS

Departure date/time: *Return date/time:*

Route/destination: *Terrain and features (river, sea, woods, etc.):*

Distance covered:

Avg. tempo: 0

1   3
                6
     2
5   4   9
   7
     8
          10

External weather

Internal weather

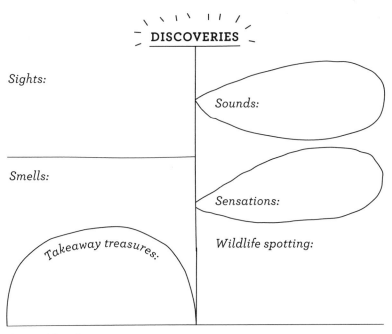

DISCOVERIES

Sights:

Sounds:

Smells:

Sensations:

Takeaway treasures:

Wildlife spotting:

Notes/sketches:

Gratitude and insights:

The Mindfulness Project, founded by Autumn Totton and Alexandra Frey, is a platform for teaching and spreading mindfulness. From its center in London, The Mindfulness Project offers a range of courses, including drop-in sessions, workshops, eight-week programs, seminars and nature-connection retreats – some available online and on location. Learn more at: _londonmindful.com_

Also available from The Mindfulness Project:

"An essential guide to mindfulness, filled with tools and practices that can enhance our well-being."
Ariana Huffington

The interactive guide that teaches mindfulness through creative exercises – accompanied by the _I am here now_ audio track by Tara Brach.

Available now throughout the world.